P.O.W.: Prisoners of Work

P.O.W.: Prisoners of Work

L. A. Girouard

VANTAGE PRESS
New York

FIRST EDITION

Published by Vantage Press, Inc.
516 West 34th Street, New York, New York 10001

Manufactured in the United States of America
ISBN: 0-533-13262-2

Library of Congress Catalog Card No.: 99-95008

0 9 8 7 6 5 4 3 2 1

To John, Kristen, and Karlie, my family and source of encouragement. For your understanding and patience as I moved through various career choices, thank you. For your conversations and contributions when I needed to test ideas, thank you.

Contents

Foreword

In generations past the workplace had a formal atmosphere. The managers were referred to as Mister Smith, or the like, and he returned the courtesy to his employees by addressing them as Mr. Jones or Miss Clancy. When Mr. Smith began addressing Miss Clancy as "Jane," Mr. Smith soon was called "Jack." Barriers and formalities in the workplace started to deteriorate. The new relaxed standards led to countless litigations, testing theories of equal rights, discrimination, and sexual harassment. Relaxed office standards continue to grow with a generation of workers who grew up with many of their own peers as role models, and we are on the crest of another change in the atmosphere of the workplace.

This book is not about what men's and women's roles are in the workplace. It does not center on women's rights, or on the existence of "good old boy" networks. Believe it or not, it's about common sense, courtesy, workplace protocol, and issues facing workers today, beyond

2000. The goal in publishing these views is to poke fun at ourselves as people, bringing the comical to the ridiculous, and to bring some sense to the continuously changing workplace. It is also intended to present some situations that may be familiar to you and provide some assistance in dealing with the pressures of working. Pass with us through the following pages and reflect on those situations that you find yourself facing in your own experiences. You may be asking yourself, "Why do we need another book on common sense issues?" Let's face it, the electronic age and corporate environments are causing more barriers to tumble. Relationships between men and women are becoming even less formal, and rules between boss and employee still need to be defined, especially in today's changing environment.

More importantly, people are changing with each new generation in such undefined manners that they don't even know what to call the current age entering the workforce. Some are termed "Generation X" and others are "Generation Next." The new work order is from the international sector, whether raised domestically in the United States or from countries around the world. They are all here to stay.

Acknowledgments

The Quality College, Orlando, Florida; Farr Associates, Greensboro, N.C.; American Management Association, New York; *Webster's New World Dictionary, Second College Edition*.

Reference to material is strictly through knowledge learned. Dictionary quotations are taken from *Webster's New World Dictionary, Second College Edition*.

Quotations or similar wording that may appear in other printed material is coincidental.

Personal Acknowledgments:

Kristen Cotnoir, for relating her experience as input into this document.

Sunny Cook, for early participation in defining subject material.

To the many co-workers through the years

who are really the subject material for the contents related. We're all human and there was never one person all so bad as may have been depicted in this book.

To past critics of my writing skills, what you see is what you get.

P.O.W.: Prisoners of Work

Age of Redemption

Put yourself in the following circumstances and imagine how you would respond in your current workplace.

You are a young man and you notice your female boss leaning over her personal computer, rubbing her neck. Do you:

1. Walk over to her and massage her shoulders while you ask a question you need answered.
2. Make no comment and walk away.
3. Speak to her and ask if this is a bad time to talk.
4. Walk away and tell your associates the boss is in a mood.
5. Don't go near her.

You are a young woman and you want to tell a joke you heard to a group of associates. You know there are sexual overtones to the joke. Do you:

1. Tell the joke.
2. Ask if anyone minds if you tell the joke.
3. Decide it's better left between close friends and refrain from telling the joke.

Depending on the background and the decade they were born in, the sad part is that there are people who would select any one of the possible answers to both questions. Many would argue that the answer is that "it depends." Certainly that is the very issue brought into courtrooms year after year. We suggest that there is a new evolution proceeding amiss with a further breakdown of traditional values. A new generation approaches that more closely links humans as humans, with little thought to male/female protocol. This new wave in evolution will sweep into the formal workplace protocol as well. Formality, gender, and position differentiation are yielding to cohesive work groups. Old ways are being pushed aside for equal recognition and quality of life values. People no longer live to work; rather, they work to afford the comforts of life and recreations that bring more enjoyment to their existence.

Because of this shift in personal values, job applicants now interview companies more frequently for satisfaction in meeting their own needs and wishes. Applicants are less restricted by geographical location than their ancestors had been. If local companies can't accommodate the ambitious beginners, they are apt to seek employment anywhere in the world. If job applicants can't have their needs met by local employers, whether those needs are for position, benefits, time off, salary, or working conditions, there is a new tendency to relocate great distances from one's place of birth.

With world expansion in the marketplace, the young talented professionals can negotiate their salary and benefits packages with potential employers. It may be true that the courts continue to protect employer rights to fire people "at will," but the negotiation process of hiring is opening up to creation of flexible employee packages. Leisure time, salary, hours, benefits, and promotional schedules are among negotiable hiring agreements. You won't see all of them in contracts, but these very issues are deciding factors in employment decisions. The younger generations will continue to push and break down old traditions in work hiring practices, when work is acceptable, and within the relationships they form.

Being in a position to negotiate job benefits doesn't come to the vast majority of workers. Most of us must live under the accepted rules of the organization for salary and benefits. Regardless of what we read about in the business magazines, the world isn't changing in such a way that it impacts all levels of the workforce. The truth is that most people fall into the category of geographically stable noncontract workers simply for the benefit and will of any organization that employs. But there is that small percentage of new professionals, who can, and do, for whatever reasons, draft their own script in the workforce. It's not only the highly intelligent or super computer wizards who seem to be in a position to do this. Sometimes it's just the person with a little more ambition, personal persuasiveness, or attitude who is able to rise above and have the guts to ask, or expect, more from those from whom they seek employment. This is the new professional we speak of and the numbers are growing.

The younger professional is more aggressive, less familiar with formal structure, and stresses independence from bureaucratic procedures. We're in the midst of creating new paradigms to stretch the boundaries of job descriptions and conventional thinking. The younger generations are becoming bolder in their actions with no distinction between gender when communicating with each other. Their behavior doesn't evince prejudice against others because of the sex or color of their co-workers, as so many generations have before us. Old prejudices may always be around, but there is definitely a shift away from them in many offices. We may very well be entering the age of redemption.

Redemption will come with quick action against workplace transgressions in the form of open communication. The boldness of the young will end old thinking to such degrees that old court records of discrimination cases will be comical and ridiculous reading to future generations.

Young men are more open to close relationships and think nothing of putting an arm around a female co-worker's shoulder, joking on various subjects, while still considering themselves to be acting professionally with no intent of wrongdoing.

Young women are bolder and less apt to remain silent in any situation. The new working women recognize inappropriate behavior and tend to address it on the spot. They're more prone to admonish openly a person who presents an uncomfortable situation. You may hear comments such as, "Listen, Bozo, you do that, or say that, again and you won't know what hit you."

The younger generations are pulled closer

together in both socioeconomic and educational situations. With many single parent or dual parent jobholders, our children are bonding in young peer groups. When these young people enter the work force, the bonding mechanisms work the same as in their high school or college years. Traditional taboos on open discussion concerning sexual exploits, jokes, and personal ribbing just won't seem to exist between office associates as in the past. There may still be some distinction between position and rank. However, there may be some relaxing of those traditions as companies trek down the downsizing path.

Reflect for a moment on the television programs that have become popular in the last few years, such as *Thirtysomething,* or *Seinfeld, Mad About You,* and *Ellen.* Each demonstrates the importance of how peer bonding has impacted society. Appearances by family members on these programs are few or very brief when they do occur. More than likely family members only have access through the telephone for a quick conversation. The conversation follows more like a status report and sounds something like this: Yes, Mom, I won't forget to send out those thank-you cards; yes, I did call Dad and wished him a happy birthday; how is he anyway, yes, yes, I did talk to him, why do you ask?

Should we then be so surprised that the values evolving in the workplace are not any different from the changing values in society?

Courtesy, Conflict, Command

In the work environment, relationships are the strongest personal assets we can collect. Keep in mind the general theory of keeping an eye on those you pass on the way up, because you just might meet them on the way down. Don't disassociate yourself from people for the wrong reasons. The best avoidance of relationship traps in ladder-climbing is not to plot your every move. Be honest with yourself and others, and courteous to everyone, not only to upper management.

Genuine courtesy is not outdated. Genuine feelings are recognized in human behavior as always. If you're not being honest or sincere when relating to others, it usually shows through. So, the least anyone can do is be courteous in the face of adversity. That in itself is enough to drive some people crazy, especially when you're being nice to someone who is antagonizing you.

Being polite does not imply backing down

from presenting your point of view. If, for example, a discussion in a meeting becomes argumentative and it appears that the one who speaks the loudest is swaying decisions his/her way, this is the time when it takes calm persuasiveness and guts to jump into the conversation. If it becomes obvious that just speaking isn't enough, try a sudden action. Move around the room to a strategic position. Acknowledge the louder person's position and congratulate the team for pulling together behind it. It's important not to put the other person down. Indicate that you know his/her plan will work. Then quickly ask everyone to listen to something else that might also work. Very often you'll find that your greatest ally is the louder speaker. If you found merit in his/her proposal, quite often the gesture is returned. In fact, solicit that person's impression first from the group. This avoids him/her from sitting back and feeling betrayed by associates if any speak up in favor of your ideas. Asking for your opponent's position first also gets your associates off the hook from choosing sides, or going with rank versus reason.

Lead the discussion toward compromise if you immediately recognize deadlock and/or closed minds. Acknowledge where the other person's plan complements your position. Again solicit the opponent's opinion. If you're getting some support and discussion continues, you're on the right track.

Well, that last scenario was picture perfect. Unfortunately, real life doesn't always work that way. Yes, those unbending people are still out there and sometimes there are no-win situations. Now you're faced with supporting a position or action that you don't really believe will work. All your barriers come alive. You're angry and others may or may not know it. Depending on your personality, your feelings may have been verbalized, but if you're an introverted thinker, you may have held your tongue. But you can be sure the reaction is the same internally. You're upset! In this situation some basic instincts are:

- Withdraw from supporting the project.
- Or you'll wait until something goes wrong, then remind people what should have happened.
- Or you may look for ways to sabotage the effort.
- Maybe you won't pull your weight of the work.
- Or, you'll do the work but complain all the way to the end.

Of course these are not career-building alternatives to choose. If you're reading this looking for what you should do in this situation, good, because we have a position. The best thing to do is grin and bear it, but, do everything you can to make the effort a success. Leaders are born making the impossible, possible. Very often you lose the battle but not the war. You might have to fall back from the front lines and reposition your thoughts and actions to supporting something you're not fully in favor of with the same vigor you would have had on your own ideas.

Because of your earlier position, you may be the first to recognize where something is going wrong.

Regroup the troops and implement some of your previous ideas. We hate to fall back on clichés, but the truth is that you need to be a team player, a true company person. You owe it to your employer to make the company successful. Sometimes that takes a lot of compromising on your part. You'll get personal rewards by letting your natural talents lead the way, instead of your emotions. The important thing to remember here is to be courteous through conflict, to remain in command of your situation.

If you find you're always beating your head against a stone wall and your ideas are never accepted, and you just can't support other ways of doing things, then get out. Sounds easy! Not in a world of tough economies and corporate downsizing. If you can't just quit this job and move on, how can you get out? Later in this book, you may find some of these answers.

The Arena of Office Politics

What is office politics? We've never seen any clear definition of it, but we recognize it when we see it, don't we? When someone gets a promotion in the office, comments about his or her political affiliation within the company abound. You hear, "Well, she was a good politician to get that job," or "He kissed every cheek along the way to get that job."

Or, have you noticed the rising stars in your office vying for position, rank, and recognition? Sometimes you can't tell if it's politics or a boxing arena.

Rising stars may hold back information from their immediate supervisors until the timing is right for them to shine. Their political instincts tell them it's time when higher-ranking managers are present to ensure proper recognition. It may be a time when they create a formal document and you notice copies have been distributed to several department managers. After all, the office politician knows whom to associate with, whom to copy on memos, how to get

AND IN THIS CORNER THE RISING STAR
HOLDS
BACK IMPORTANT INFORMATION TO
SHINE
ANOTHER DAY. THAT'S AN
UNEXPECTED JAB
FOR OUR DEFENDING CHAMP OF
YESTERYEAR.

recognition, and to what committees to volunteer his or her time.

Look up the word "politics" in the dictionary, and you'll find some of the following definitions:

1. Science of government
2. Political affairs
3. Political methods, tactics
4. Political opinions
5. Factional scheming for power

The definition of "politician" in your dictionary may read:

> "One actively engaged in politics: often used with implications of seeking personal partisan gain, scheming, etc. . . ."

Stopping at the first definition can still leave you confused as to the true meaning of politics. Let's get right to the heart of politics. Politics is scheming for power, personal or in representation of a larger body. The word "faction" in the dictionary further explains political behavior.

1. "A group of people in an organization working in a common cause against the main body."

2. "Dissension"

No wonder we all get a little uneasy when we recognize political activity within the office. Those people who are rocking the boat are change agents. What they're doing is going to have positive and negative effects on others around them. Some of us are going to work harder to compete in the arena and some of us are going to be knocked out before the fifteenth round. Some of us are going to place our bet on the rising star and the rest of us will resist them and the change they represent. After the final bell, some of us will be left to just continue daily going through the motions without daring to get into the ring again.

You can recognize those in your office who weren't knocked out, but were declared the loser by the judge's ballot. They're the people coasting or creating tactics for causing small bodies of dissenting workers. These people ar-

Corporate goal: Quality Improvement
Negative leadership results: obstacles to quality, and dissenting workers.

en't even defending champions any longer; they're filling time until retirement.

Who are these people and what do they look like? In some offices they might be the people you've seen bounced from position to position, up, down, and sideways within the organization. They tend to have somewhat of a negative attitude and each year it gets stronger. Company-sponsored programs are usually welcomed with comments like, "Here we go again, another two-year brainwashing scheme that will get a lot of time and energy, then go away. Why don't they just put the money in our paycheck? That'll motivate us more than the latest buzzwords in corporate America."

We see these people everywhere in the workforce. You might have seen them in the department stores or in restaurant service. These people tend to have lost the customer service attitude of a friendly helpful spirit and taken on the persona of Clint Eastwood as Dirty Harry. You know the expression on their face tells you that they're thinking, *Go ahead, make my day.* But you attempt to communicate with them anyway, being the customer and all, and ask them a question. What? No reaction, no answer, or did they just point a finger in another direction, or did they just grab your plate without a word and bring it to the kitchen? Yeah, that's pretty much the kind of reaction we see out there. In this situation, we usually become friendlier to these people and thank them and let them know they've been very helpful. This is great to do just to see the expression on their faces.

Avoiding Political Blunders

If you're not plotting your own personal agenda, and you honestly want to do the right thing, keep the following close at hand. Pull this section out if you have to and post it so you can read it over and over again.

1. Never contradict your boss in public.

2. Never copy controversial correspondence originating above your boss's position without permission.

3. Think about whom you are copying on electronic correspondence.

4. Never take a salesperson's side when your boss is questioning the product, service, or price.

5. Don't over argue a point of view.
6. Don't talk about your co-workers negatively.
7. Support your team members if someone is complaining about them to you.
8. Keep your boss aware of problems.
9. Be willing to admit when you're wrong.
10. Be willing to say, "I don't know."
11. Be willing to say, "I made a mistake."
12. Don't contradict your boss during meetings.
13. Tell your boss your position in private when it differs from his/hers.
14. Ask your boss to represent your position as well as his/hers.
15. Support the people whom you may supervise.

16. Be open to others' suggestions.

17. Be willing to listen, as well as to be heard.

"We can't all be right! Listen, let's put all our ideas on the board and see what develops!"

On the Inside

Every day there are little things that happen on the inside of the office that is just outside of what makes up your job. It's the one factor that accounts for most interruptions, loss of productivity, and lack of order. The one ingredient is other people. You remember what they look like! They're the less robotic things that walk, talk, have feelings, opinions, and urgent needs. Yes, they're the people you work with every day.

Protocol and procedures need to be emphasized every few years just to remind people that there is more going on than what affects them. Did I say every few years? People need reminders every day! Reminders of what is proper in the office need to be emphasized every day because people forget every day. People are struggling to get a job done, and all too often they just forget the do's and don'ts of working in an office.

Calling over office walls, entering offices where it is obvious that meetings are going on, and cutting into other phone conversations all seem more commonplace these days. Do people really need to be reminded what is proper behavior? Yes. So for those who need reminding:

1. Don't enter conversations over an office wall.

2. Don't enter an office where you see other people meeting unless you are invited.

3. If you hear someone on the phone and just have the urge to add something to the conversation, don't.

4. If you see two people talking in a hall, don't stop. Keep walking unless they stop you. Silent greeting is acceptable.

5. Don't read mail from someone's in-box while you're waiting for him to get off the phone.

6. Never pick up anything from someone's desk unless it is offered.

7. Never take anything from another person's office to borrow without their knowledge. Leave a note if it is urgent.

8. Never enter an office while someone is on the phone and just stand there until he or she gets off.

9. If someone is engrossed in operating a calculator or computer terminal, don't interrupt unless it is obvious that a break in thought has occurred.

10. When in doubt, think it out, before going to another person to ask for help or to put a question.

11. If you enter an officc, don't try to read what is on the person's desk or computer terminal while you're in conversation with him/her.

"Forgive our faults, we're only human!"

Personnel Conflict or Taming of the Crew

Why do companies spend thousands of dollars every year on quality improvement programs, management by objective processes, leadership development, and countless other efforts to promote teamwork?

Is it to correct some basic flaw in human nature? What is that flaw? Is it lack of discipline, apathy, or just plain personality conflicts that prevent people from working well together? Do companies spend millions in training just to resolve personal conflicts?

You bet!

While some will argue that apathy and conflict are symptoms of a larger problem, perhaps even with management, companies aren't willing to point the finger at themselves. None of the nominal group exercises we've experienced get to the heart of the problem. You know the technique! A group gets together and writes down the answer to questions posed by the group leader. The answers are then all put down where everyone can view them, and then they are grouped into similar categories. The group then prioritizes the categories according to importance. When this technique is used to identify obstacles to quality, and only symptoms appear, chances are people are not being honest about what they feel the real problem is, and that prevents quality. If you have experienced one of these sessions, you may have reached the same conclusion.

By the way, this nominal group technique is an excellent tool to get everyone involved in providing input, especially those introverts we talked about earlier, because the ideas are written down first in silent thought and then handed into the facilitator of the meeting. No one has to feel afraid of offering an unpopular idea or letting feelings on subjects show through. Importantly, we don't have to worry about offending another worker with a different point of view and causing an uneasy situation to occur. The truth is that most hostile situations are really based on personal feelings that dwell in each of us.

A lot of our personal feelings (we'll call stuff) get in the way of maintaining harmonious work environments. We carry stuff from childhood as learned experiences as to how we interact with each other and react to various circumstances. This stuff lies deep within our core to escape as defenses against outside attacks, protecting our egos and warding off all perceptions of harm. We are complicated creatures that require taming. Taming comes about through some of the classes our companies put us through to ward off the stuff we've carried deep in our psyches. Our egos recognize what companies are doing and we pretend to free our stuff and hide it a little deeper. But our stuff is there waiting. Waiting for the one-on-one battle with another person's stuff. And thus, personal conflict is born.

Conflict in and of itself is not bad in an organization. It is indicative of a dynamic environment and work teams that are willing to share ideas. Conflict is a good tool to encourage freethinking and open visionary boundaries. Redesigning techniques used in reshaping corporate core competencies today stresses thinking outside the traditional box and looking beyond what the company is doing today. Those involved then must focus on what they do well, and improve, sell, or eliminate what is failing. This process often yields new opportunities and changes throughout the workplace. Conflict plays an important role in an organization if all participants share ideas openly and without fear of personal harm as a result of unacceptable notions. These strategy sessions are usually the first step to making revolutionary changes for the organization.

Traditionally, people don't handle change very well. There is something unknown; it's fearful to not know how change will affect us personally. It is not in our nature to be comfortable with new ideas, new ways of doing our jobs, and learning philosophies of effective teamwork. After all, we all think we're individuals. We know what is best for ourselves!

Proponents of change are thought of as opportunity seekers, political animals, corporate rodents, and just plain troublemakers. Change agents must prove themselves over and over again and obtain sustained successes to their credit. Only after proving themselves do change agents receive positive titles in our minds. They become visionaries, geniuses, corporate heroes, and people we see as those whose coattails might make for a good ride.

Those who don't survive change, struggle, but continue to fight old battles and eventually lose respect of those around them. It doesn't matter how many corporate-sponsored programs are initiated; not all of the people will jump on board to get with the team. Conflict is an inevitable result.

Personalities that Cause Conflict

The causes of conflict can be many within an organization. A major source of conflict can originate within corporate management itself over how the company is directed, the culture, the attitudes, and how people are traditionally treated in certain situations. Perhaps these come about through major changes, such as mergers and downsizing, or in how the company helps or ignores personal problems of their employees. Some companies recognize when a person is going through a difficult time and will allow the person a little slack for a while to allow him or her to recover. Other companies will show force to get the person to jump right back into work or fire them for poor performance.

The "Caesar" type of manager is a major factor in the origin of conflict. Some thrive on setting up situations that cause conflict. Typically this type of manager will pit two people against each other to see how each performs. It is similar to sending the Christians into the

Coliseum to battle the lions. The Caesar manager loves the conflict and feeds it with comments to both persons about how they can learn from each other. The combatants are each told this separately of course. They're never in the same room together when Caesar is telling them about each other. The Caesar tells you the bad points of the other person. You know that the other person is being told about your faults as well. The Caesar manager always uses power against you, pumping up his own self-worth. He/she reminds you who's in control, and has influence over your future, your salary, and your performance reviews.

The office "weasel" typically is the pawn the boss uses to cause other forms of conflict within the office. The weasel is the person who tries to undermine activities that you are working on or managing. The weasel is the person who sends memos concerning your department and doesn't have the courtesy to copy you on the memo. The weasel is the person who holds secret meetings to discuss areas you are responsible for and then uses the information in a more important meeting with upper management present, often presenting the material as his/her own. The weasel is the person who accuses you of not being a team player when his/her actions are against the true spirit of teamwork. The weasel notices who doesn't have the ear of the boss and repeats that person's words after a good idea was presented when it fell on deaf ears. The boss then praises the weasel for coming up with the idea and the weasel gladly accepts credit.

The "wannabe" is the person who wants to get to the top any way he/she can. This person doesn't have the weasel instincts but rather the straightforward approach of wanting that top job no matter what. This person is knowledgeable and will go right to the top to point out the shortcomings of the department in general, and its people, and make many suggestions to change the environment. It doesn't matter whom they step on to get there. The wannabe is self-absorbed, has little contact with the little people, and always avoids eye contact unless the other person is at the highest levels in the organization. The wannabe has few friends and conflict exists only at the lower levels because employees know the power of the wannabe at higher levels. Unfortunately for the wannabes, they are often used by upper management for their knowledge and eventually burn out by overextending their knowledge.

The "bull" is the person in the office who sees red whenever things don't go his way. He leaps and bounds from his office at the slightest thing he doesn't like, when an idea is not according to his thinking, or when something goes wrong. The bull tells his staff whom to talk to and whom not to talk to in the organization. The bull selects people to support and attacks everyone else. This person causes widespread conflict, not just the one-on-one type, but conflict between groups.

The "defenders" also cause conflict because they are typically not "yes" people. Defenders could keep the peace if only they would keep their mouths shut when they perceive that they are being attacked. The defender stands up against what is wrong and tries to point out injustices. If only the defender would agree all the time, life would be so much simpler for the bull, the weasel, and the wannabe. Unfortunately, the defender would then be known as the mouse, and certainly would have no self-respect, nor the respect of others in the organization.

The "gladiators" can be managers or key personnel who have influence on the floor. They genuinely see where justice must prevail and stir up the crowd and the rumor mill. They can cause conflict but not in a threatening situation. They will typically adapt to the winning leaders in any battle for power. They will then become gladiators for the righteousness of the new leadership in time.

The "aristocrat" manager is the social type who knows everyone in the organization and knows all the buzzwords to converse on just about any topic. The aristocratic manager reads a lot about the organization, everyone's status report, and just spends a great deal of time mingling throughout the day. The aristocrat gives the impression of having good management skills to peers and upper management. To those reporting to the aristocrat, there is no direction other than to just have them bring problems forward. The aristocrat looks for equality but only to the extent that someone, or other groups are not getting more than themselves or their team. Most people like the aristocrat unless they have been the targets in an equality war.

The "spectator" manager is the person who just wants to be part of the crowd. He or she searches the room for the strongest, the one who, it appears, will come out ahead and then begins to agree with whatever that person proposes. This person has a strong need to belong and wants to be there for life. The spectator doesn't like change, but will accept change where he/she is most comfortable. The spectator doesn't make waves in the organization and tends to be people oriented. He or she makes up for lack of leadership by being nice, presenting gifts, and holding coffees just to impart good will. The spectator manager will typically look to have at least two strong gladiators at his side whom he can rely on to present projects and objectives. The conflict that the spectator managers tend to cause is within their own teams as those under them attempt to come out from the bleachers.

Affiliate managers just want to be part of the crowd. They got their positions through their social contacts with other managers. You might think of them as the social butterfly. The affiliate manager is different than the aristocratic manager in that they don't have the killer instinct. He or she doesn't intentionally go after people but are influential in having people go after other people. They're prominent at all social gatherings, making the right contacts as they work the crowd, and always have interesting things to say to the person they're addressing. The affiliate manager avoids conflict in meetings, only takes sides in private, and can appear to be a peace-maker for management. But, behind the scenes, this manager can really stir the pot to bring problems from a simmer to a boil. At the boiling point, the affiliate will typically feign innocence and move on to other topics.

Surviving Through Conflict

You first need to recognize the type of conflict you're engaged in to determine what you should do to survive. Healthy people can disagree on a subject and continue to work well together. But what do you do in unhealthy situations?

First, it won't be easy! If your manager doesn't recognize the situation or refuses to do anything about it, you have a tough battle ahead. If you're not willing to move on to something new, you need to develop buffers between you and the source of conflict. Buffers can take the shape of physical relocation, other people representing your position, or internal transfers.

The most dangerous choice is having others represent your position to someone you are in conflict with. After all, they are not you, and the mere fact that they are compatible with the implied adversary creates further gaps in communication. Your presenter may favor opposing views more readily than you would. This type of relationship is, at best, on shaky ground. It can only tumble one way or the other. In other words, you'll survive and they won't, or, vice versa. Don't you hate it when that's the only outcome?

Survival through conflict is based on a personal choice and dependent upon a vast amount of circumstances. You can consult with a wide variety of experts, human resource officials, peers, and your personal contacts outside the company to give you advice on how to handle conflict. They will all be happy to provide you with their abundant wisdom. Some of you will check with all these sources, depending upon your internal method of reaching decisions.

There is no one way to survive conflict other than doing what is right for you. Trust your instincts. But do something to avoid prolonged negative relationships and situations. We know some of you are getting ready to close the book on what you're reading, but we guarantee you're going to find this interesting. Because:

1. You're not sure where we're going.

2. You're waiting to find a category to relate to.

3. You're a control-oriented type and in

Resolving a conflict can be as easy as initiating a phone call between all parties involved.

the end you just want to make sure you're right.

4. You're the analytical type and you want more data.

5. You're the social type and you want to learn how to keep the peace.

6. You're the aggressive type and want to learn what others are learning to counter political scheming with your own new tactics.

Whatever your motivation is in reading this book, there is something you're seeking; to survive in an ever-changing environment. Importantly, knowing how to relate to others in a positive and productive manner is the cornerstone of successful business people, and you do want to be successful.

Our inner orientation toward control, aggressiveness, social ability, and analysis are some of the strengths that drive us. The combination of these strengths with other traits, such as extroverted or introverted thinking, visionary characteristics, and our ability toward perceptive or judgmental deductions, are all part of the stuff we carry that makes us unique individuals. Our very strengths, taken to extreme, can work against us to become our weakest links leading to failure. We're neither expert in the field of psychology nor teachers of self-actualization techniques. Our message is that the first step to understanding others is to understanding yourself. Invest the time to test your own personality profile through formal testing. There are professionals available in your community or through your workplace who can assist you. The experience and the knowledge you receive are the first steps to surviving conflict. You may be surprised to learn that the conflict is only within you and has nothing to do with others around you.

One thing is sure; you can't change other people. You can change how you deal with them.

Internal Power Plays

Did you ever see those signs in department stores that say: "When things go right, tell others, but when things go wrong, tell us"? There is a lot in this saying that should be taken into the workplace and given thought to whenever you encounter a negative situation. Many of us can relate to a situation when something we're responsible for has a glitch in its operation. Seldom do the persons experiencing a problem report it directly to the people responsible for fixing it. Somewhere in the frustration of people's minds, their common sense breaks down and communication protocol goes out the window. What do they do? They call the highest person in your organization who then starts a boulder rolling downhill. Sometimes days go by with a lot of executives discussing what could have gone wrong. They finally bring the issue to the person responsible for fixing the situation, and it is fixed in a very short time. This can only mean that if the person with the frustration had called the right person in the first place, the problem could have been cleared up without a lot of wasted productivity in the executive branch.

There is something very basic going on here! People don't think about doing what is right when they are under stress. People don't give any thought to other people when they are in an uncomfortable situation. They just want the problem fixed, and they don't care how it gets fixed. The first instinct is to go to the top of the management ladder.

What we find more frustrating is when a problem is pointed out from the top in another department. There is an unwritten rule that executives will only speak to other executives. Well, the last thing the manager of your department wants to hear from one of his peers is that something is wrong in what his department is producing. We're always amazed at the agility and level of activity these managers display in getting to the bottom of the matter. Meetings are called, formal edicts are distributed, memos start flying, and the list goes on. We suggest that there are better ways for people to work on problems.

When things go wrong, tell the people closest to the solution first. Where is it written that the Vice President of Marketing can't talk to the

Supervisor of Manufacturing? Instead we waste time with power plays to attack problems. Many service organizations establish help desks to handle calls from internal customers from other departments or remote office locations. Very often we find that the issues brought to the attention of top management have not even been reported to the help desk for problem reporting and tracking. In such situations, there is a tendency to put the people responsible for the issue in a defensive attitude when the problem finally reaches them. They feel under attack rather than having been trusted to receive the information first and to find the corrective action.

Those considering going to the top with any issue can go a long way toward achieving good communication by giving thought to who is directly responsible for the issue, prior to bringing it to levels sometimes two to three times higher than where it should be reported. If time is taken to let the right people know of the problem, you are showing them that you trust them to report the problem upward themselves. Be up front with the person and let him/her know how serious you consider the problem and that if it can't be resolved in an expected timeframe, you'd like to have the problem-solving escalated. Request feedback or a report on how close the issue stands toward resolution by a particular date. Most of all don't be a power player when dealing with problems; it only makes the problem bigger. Power players may get their problem resolved, but they lose respect from those who are trying to help them. And habitual complainers, finger pointers, and power players put the support personnel on the defensive as their morale begins to deteriorate.

Just Plain Old Courtesy

People in a customer service role, whether in a department store or in an organization's internal support department, take more abuse from their "customers" than anyone should have to in today's educated world. It is amazing the number of rude stories we hear about in this environment. People must really believe that if they yell at, swear at, or threaten the customer service person they're going to get faster service, or the problem fixed sooner. But as discussed earlier, frustration displayed by one party just causes resentment and maybe some reluctance to accommodate the complaining party.

One such story was encountered by a retail store assistant manager. A customer expecting delivery of merchandise early one morning stayed home to receive the order. As time passed and no delivery came, she got on the phone to the retail store and rudely hit into the assistant manager with vulgar language and threats. The threats didn't stop with simply stating that she would return the order, but included sending her husband to the store, who by the way is not as patient as she. The assistant manager at first was on the defensive and stated that if the person felt so strongly, to just send it back because it would be resold before the day was out. Then, remembering that the person probably did make some personal sacrifice to be home, the assistant manager changed to a gentler tone of voice. She offered to call the independent delivery service that the store used to find out what the problem was with the day's schedule and promised to call the customer right back. She learned that the delivery truck had broken down and immediately returned the customer call.

The assistant manager told the customer that the truck had broken down and explained to the customer that she really hit into the delivery service for not notifying the store of a delay. The assistant manager made it perfectly clear that the delivery had to get there within two hours even if they had to send another truck. "After all, it's not the delivery service's reputation that is on the line, it's our store's so if they're not there in two hours, will you promise to call me back?" The customer was so struck that someone else was fighting for her that she immediately spoke to the assistant manager with more respect and apologized for her earlier outburst.

The lesson here is to turn the tide in uncomfortable situations. Of course, the outcome must be positive with the promised action to follow. You can always be nice to people, but unless the promised action follows, you're only giving lip service. People must see results to regain the confidence—in the store in this case, or in an organization's customer service department or help desk.

Within a company, for example, if your job is to take calls all day at a help desk and you act very professionally even with irate calls, the caller will become even more irate if nothing happens even with the nicest telephone mannerisms.

One example occurred at a personal computer help desk. After one week of working with the technical people, an office manager called screaming at a technical person to find someone else to get the problem fixed if it couldn't be resolved by him. Before giving the technical person the opportunity to escalate the problem, the office manager called two management levels higher to complain that there was always a problem with working with this technician. When the situation was brought to the technician's supervisor, the truth came out that the people in the office were not literate enough with PC's to troubleshoot the problem over the phone. The more they tried to fix the problem, the worse it became, because PC-start up files were being changed erroneously. The supervisor backed up the technician, who suggested the purchase of PC cloning software, which allows remote access to another person's PC and gives full control of the remote PC to the technician. The technician today gets high praises from internal customers because he has a direct view into that remote PC and can pinpoint the problem and correct it himself.

The reason for the turnaround here was the fact that the point of frustration was eliminated. Business people want to work on business problems and not technical problems. When something external to their particular job becomes a deterrent for getting the job done, the pressure mounts to a boiling point and people in this situation literally don't care whom they may hurt. Unfortunately, this is human nature and all the professionalism in the world will never change everyone. So customer service people need to be tough skinned and psychologists in addition to being courteous, professional, and knowing how to get their job done.

As for those on the other side of the customer service representative, try to be a little more professional in the language you choose for conveying your frustration. You are the one who initially looks bad when you choose to blow off steam or take something higher in the corporate ranks. First, before getting on the phone, count to ten. Explain the problem to yourself; calmly call the person who is to receive the problem. Ask how long it should take to resolve the matter, or find out what the next step is in the process. If you don't see action or a resolution, call the person back and ask to speak with his/her supervisor together, or on a conference call, in which all parties may participate. You'll find that working together tends to put all the pieces together much sooner.

"Hey, you folks at the help desk have just got to help me out here. Here's the problem. . . ."

How to Know When You're Plateaued

Today the competition is fierce in the work place. We're faced with a generation that is characterized as being the first to have not done better than their parents. They're hungry for success and want to succeed. With companies either downsizing, rightsizing, or outsourcing, employees are either reaching their level of incompetence faster or are being supported by consultants supplied by the outsourcing provider. The career track is changing and the elevator up often stops midway at a plateau with no doors to the top floors. Company-hopping is slowing down because the jobs are not opening up. So, what do you do if you're suddenly plateaued at your job?

Do you:

1. Seek professional counseling.

2. Become an office politician.

3. Go back to school to learn a new field.

4. Live with it, get over it, and cash your paycheck weekly.

5. Complain about it and do nothing.

6. Encourage your company to cross train.

Those are your choices. There is no right answer for everyone. Where you might pick choices one and three, someone else might choose number four. The point here is to recognize when you have few options available for career growth.

The next step is to determine what that means to you personally. You're the decision-maker when it comes to what to do next. You may want to complete a career choice work sheet to help you decide what's right for you. You can create your own from the sample provided and include additional questions that are pertinent to your situation.

How to Know When I'm Plateaued and What to Do about It/Worksheet

I. AM I PLATEAUED? (ANSWER YES OR NO)

1. Have you been in the same job more than five years?

2. Do you have the knowledge to move laterally within your company?

3. Do positions open up every two to three years?

4. Are you a likely candidate for your supervisor's position?

5. Is your supervisor within ten years of retirement?

6. Is your supervisor in favor with management?

The higher number of No answers the more you are plateaued.

II. DO I CARE ABOUT BEING PLATEAUED?

1. Do you like the job you are doing?

2. Do you want to be in management?

3. Do you like to do reports, administrative work, and attend meetings?

4. Do you like putting in extra time at the job?

5. Do you mind putting in extra time at work?

6. Do you get jealous when others are promoted?

7. Do you take extra classes to learn more?

8. Did you complete extra classes once in the present job?

9. Do you volunteer for projects or special committees?

10. Do you apply for posted job openings within your company?

11. Do you know you're likely to fill the next position in your organization chart, but it's unlikely to be available for more than five years, and it bothers you?

A high number of YES answers means you care about being plateaued. If you care, go on to the next step. Remember you are now the decision-maker answerable only to yourself.

III. NOW THAT I CARE ABOUT BEING PLATEAUED, WHAT CAN I DO?

1. Can I update my résumé and send it to other companies?

2. Can I apply for management positions

in other companies with my experience record?

3. Am I young enough to start a new pension credit at another company?

4. Do I want to start a new career in a different field?

5. Am I willing to return to school?

6. Do I want to start my own business?

7. Do I have the capital to start my own business?

8. Can I get investors to start my own business?

9. Do I have the knowledge to start my own business?

10. Can I get the knowledge to start my business?

11. Do I have the courage to risk a change?

12. Do I want to stay with the existing company?

13. Can I encourage cross-training programs?

14. Do I want to accept more responsibility in lieu of promotion?

15. Can I be creative and get personal satisfaction while waiting for advancement?

16. Am I in good standing with management and company directorship?

17. Can I live with the way the company is developing?

18. Can I get along with the money I earn?

19. Can I get over being plateaued?

20. Can I make a decision?

The first ten questions are intended to be thought provoking. The second ten are designed to help you reach a decision. If there are four or more "No" answers in the second set of ten questions, you should look more seriously at making a change in your career.

Remember, only you can make that decision.

WHAT DID YOU DECIDE TO DO????

If You Find Yourself Plateaued

Reaching a career plateau is not necessarily a bad thing. Some people look forward to it. There is certain comfortability in finding your niche in life, knowing that you do something well, and wanting to stay with it. The way the word "plateaued" is being used in the corporate world has a demotivating effect to many people. We believe the intent was to stress that there aren't too many fast tracks to get a head start toward a management career. Organizations are in the midst of flattening the management hierarchy so there are fewer levels of managers between the brass and the workforce. This is supposed to strengthen communication and keep people attuned to the various aspects involved in operating the business. Not enough years have passed to determine if this new strategy will succeed. We are already seeing some shift back to a more structured organization for companies that implemented a matrix reporting structure that left the organization too flat, too big, and so independent that the companies became immobilized. No names, no lawsuits. But you know who they are if you read the *Wall Street Journal.*

Technology advancements also contribute to a trend for fewer people to manage. The workforce is becoming more sophisticated in using electronic tools, with emphasis on productivity and redesigning old processes. These efforts may keep people in positions longer as manual or clerical functions are reduced.

We have always lived in a changing world, but we haven't always had personal power to change our own circumstances. The days of staying on the farm or in the same community to find rewarding work is long gone. Today we think nothing of relocating across the country or across the world to find job opportunities. We all have the personal power to decide what is best for ourselves.

We are proponents of change and suggest that each individual can find opportunity and satisfaction in career choices. The fast food, fast car, and fast paced generation may have to find patience or be willing to take more risks than their ancestors. If you're so uncomfortable in a position that it affects your productivity, attitude, health, and personal life, you owe it only to yourself to seek out and find other options.

Electronic Mail and You

The mail animal is on the loose! The beast lurks in our computer terminals now in the form of inter-office correspondence, customer direct mail through public phone access switching, and fax to terminal facilities. We're told there is no excuse for poor communication anymore. The truth is there is information overload occurring and human nature continues to maintain only selective retention of data. There is just no way we can remember everything that is mailed to us on a daily basis.

We can be away from our desks for a two-hour meeting and find there are twenty-one mail messages waiting. Depending on the size of the documents, you can easily spend your whole day reading and responding to electronic mail. With all this communication you can still come up short. How many times have you made a comment in a meeting and your boss responds with, "I sent you an e-mail on that!!?" Your only sensible reply may be that you'll read it again. And the tone in the boss's voice is questionable because he/she may not remember if the e-mail was really sent. That boss is just as confused as everyone else is because the same e-mail overload is affecting his/her performance, as well as everyone else.

Even with the e-mail explosion, we can find some entertainment or humor in the type of communication we see. Some personal favorite electronic mail is stuff received from those duking it out at the keyboard. You know them; they're the people who just left a meeting in total disagreement. Contestant number one in this game goes back and documents his position and copies everyone who was at the meeting.

Contestant number two replies with comments clearly meant to infuriate contestant one. This correspondence continues with shorter and shorter flying e-mail until,

1. a third party steps in, usually the boss, and writes "knock it off" or . . .
2. one of the contestants just stops responding.

This routine isn't very productive, but is often the source of entertainment to the others being copied.

Introverts love e-mail because they can hide in their offices and compose to their hearts'

E-mail used as a destructive tool can be as damaging as a sword through the heart.

content. The ultimate danger comes when some extrovert approaches them face to face to discuss the memo. The introvert is quick though and responds, "Let me think about it and I'll send you a memo." We also like being copied on correspondence from one introvert to another. We're always impressed with what we're reading until we realize those two sit side by side in the office. They can literally go days without talking to one another. But, we certainly are impressed with what is really on their minds, aren't we? These could be the people who never offer a verbal opinion on anything, or they could be the people who sit in a meeting and never utter a single word; then some of these people go back to the privacy of their minds and create written beauty.

Even though we can find humor in what we see occurring in office communication, we can see that there is something very basic that we're losing. We are quickly losing the value of face-to-face communication in many facets of life. Sales media is flooding our fax lines, home shopping is a popular pastime for television viewers, and banking can occur from our personal computers or push button telephones. Entertainment for many consist of home videos, electronic games, and compact disc listening. Food services can make deliveries to your front door, and shopping vans filled with groceries are gaining notoriety in some communities. The days of Sunday dinner with grandparents, aunts and uncles seem to have disappeared. Intimate family dining is quickly going by the wayside as well. Today, we could easily create an environment for ourselves in which we don't have to speak to anyone for weeks. So why should our business communication be any different?

Electronic correspondence can be a productivity tool but should not replace personal follow-up. The message you're trying to convey can get buried in tons of other messages. We have a tendency to re-file the messages to read later and then fail to do so. Electronic mail should be followed up with a personal meeting or phone call, especially if important details are at stake. Your message will be clearer to the recipient and retained with greater understanding. Salespeople have learned the same trick with following meetings or conversations with written follow-up. The reverse should be true. Written correspondence should be followed up with verbal contact.

Research has shown that we retain more in human memory when we hear information versus reading it. Millions of dollars are poured into advertising each year to send messages with memorable jingles, repetitive catchy phrases, and visual effects in the presentation of television advertising. These marketers have learned the value of supporting their product with as many visual and audio recognition aids as possible, just so that we will remember the message they're trying to convey. Inter-office correspondence is no less important and needs to be supported with the personal element of speech. We all need to keep face-to-face communication alive.

Electronic Mail Etiquette

1. Copy those people on your memos who really have a need to know.

2. Never copy above your manager unless it is known about.

3. If you are referencing work or activity conducted in another unit, it is proper to copy that department head. Copying one individual or supervisor is not sufficient.

4. Try not to use e-mail to solve personal

"Jane, about that e-mail I sent you, I meant it when I said your proposal was well done. Your projections for improvement in productivity are startling."

gripes. The impression you leave will hurt you more than the recipient.

5. E-mail is a corporate productivity tool. Avoid personal use, such as setting up golf dates or creating chain letters, or writing résumés. You can probably name other misuse better than we can.

6. Follow important correspondence with personal follow-up.

7. Follow important correspondence with personal follow-up. (It was worth repeating)

8. When forwarding e-mail onto other readers, always copy the original sender. This avoids that person being caught off guard if questioned about the document. Status reports excluded.

9. Delete old messages or re-file under appropriate electronic folders.

The Telephone, Voicemail, and You

There was a time when making a phone call was a simple thing. There was a time when reaching a person was expected. There was a time when you didn't have to listen to menu options to reach another branch of the telephone system to hear another list of options to reach the person you're trying to reach to hear his options for leaving him a message or type an alternative to reach another menu of options for immediate help where his list of options sends you back to the switchboard because all lines are busy at this time. We'll say they're busy! And the sad part is that probably not one conversation took place. Well, times have changed! And we have to change with the times.

Companies have various procedures set up at the switchboard depending on the type of business they're in and the culture the organizations want to represent to their customers. Because procedures vary from long menu options to a personal greeting and then computer interface, we're staying away from that subject. It's too explosive! We've found that in general conversation concerning telephone switchboard auto-attendants (the new term for telephone operators inside the box), intelligent people become infuriated by having to make choices presented by a computerized switchboard. Many tell us they just hang up. But for those companies out there with long menu options, we suggest take heed to the message you're sending to your customers.

As for your personal voicemail protocol, your position should be to update your greeting frequently. You should include a message that indicates if you are in or out of the office, an opportunity for the person to leave you a message, and most importantly, a way for the caller to reach a person if immediate help is needed. The biggest complaint we hear is that people don't indicate if they're going to be away from their desk for the entire day, week, month, etc. Most people don't mind leaving a message if they know they'll get a call back. The problem is when they don't, only to find out the person they left a voicemail message for was away on vacation all week. GET THE MESSAGE?

Telephone systems today allow the incoming call to jump from one phone to another if the call is not answered in a specified number of rings. They call this the "call path," and your on-site telephone administrators can program it into the central telephone system. Not all companies poll each employee for their preferred call path. We suggest researching the path your calls take and be sure you're satisfied with the procedure. Better yet, call your own phone to see how others experience trying to reach you. You may be mortified to find that the caller is hearing ten rings before the phone is answered.

Rule of thumb advice: Never let your phone jump to other telephone extensions more than once.

"If this phone isn't answered soon, I'm taking my business somewhere else."

Inter-Intra-Extra-Nets

Read all about them! The power of electronic communication has really exploded with Internet technology. Every time we turn around, there is something new added to the technology, which before anything of consequence can be published about it, could be changed. The best way to keep up with the technology and what's new about it is on the World Wide Web itself. I had just figured out the difference between Internet and Intranet when all of a sudden Extranet came on the scene. So what does this technology mean to you, and how does it fit into your work environment?

Corporate strategies to introduce the Internet technology centers on a return of profit to the organization, customer service and communication, and delivery of product or service faster than the competition. The company is interested in protection against liability from lawsuits, network hackers, disgruntled employees sending confidential data to others through the Internet, and a host of various viruses that can infiltrate a network through Internet communication. For these reasons, using the Internet in a corporate environment is typically introduced with strong guidelines and employee agreements, which outline the responsibility of the company and the employees. More importantly, these corporate agreements typically hold the company blameless if employees are offended by Internet content, if someone obtains their Internet addresses for harassment purposes, or if an employee incurs large expenses through online interaction and disclosure of personal credit cards on the Internet.

The threats are real and you must be prepared to support your company and its protection by agreeing to the terms of such agreements. Your first reaction to the agreement will most likely be not to sign it because of the ambiguous language, the strong indication of personal responsibility over content sent to and from the Internet, or because of the mystery surrounding this new electronic age. Others sign the agreement without question because they can now finally send e-mail to a brother at college or relatives around the world.

Your responsibility in using the Internet in the working environment is to use it as a tool for the betterment of the organization and to enhance personal knowledge for the betterment of the position you hold within the company. Signing on the Internet while at work should have a purpose. In other words you've been asked to research a subject, or you have a need to learn more about an organization, product, or service of another company with which you do business. Those who aimlessly go from Web site to Web site are said to be surfing the Net. Companies are concerned over lost productivity from this type of behavior, and you need to understand that lost productivity is lost money in the form or your wages, possible missed deadlines, or late in delivering a revenue-generating service or product to the customer.

We also now have the capability of instant delivery of e-mail to customers and suppliers through the use of Internet mail. It is more important now to review what you're sending. Take a moment to think about it, reread the mail, and consider the information you're attaching to the e-mail message. You are not just representing yourself now when you click on the "send" icon. What you write is now representing the company as well. What you commit to can be a binding commitment to your organization. What you send may be intended for internal distribution and the consequence of sending confidential or proprietary information can mean a large liability to your organization. If you have any doubt about something that you're sending through the Internet, it is still okay to pause and escalate a question to a person of authority within the organization.

The Internet technology, the electronic possibilities, are continually expanding and large publications and manuals abound. So while you're learning just enough to become dangerous, know how to apply the technology appropriately to avoid surprises to yourself and your organization. Surprises are the predecessors of lawsuits, lost sales, lost confidence, and lost jobs, which could possibly be your own.

Business Travel

You are traveling with co-workers to a business conference but don't really want to spend all your time with them. What do you do?

1. Find out what sessions they're attending and go to different ones.

2. Ignore telephone messages from them to meet for dinner.

3. Pretend you don't know them when you meet them during the week.

4. Arrange your schedule to meet for dinner most nights and let them know you've made some personal plans while you're at the conference.

Well, you've guessed it! Many would prefer to put themselves through the stress of acting out 1 through 3 instead of being honest with their business associates. The right thing to do sometimes seems so hard for people to choose. Just as when you're traveling with your family, it is common sense to let co-workers know of your personal plans. They may not love you like your family does, but just disappearing can cause some feelings of abandonment or needless worry by your associate about what's going on with you.

As for your actions and attitudes during the week, if you choose any of the first three choices, you'll be feeling some guilt. You'll be constantly looking over your shoulder and basically you'll lose a lot of the conference and your private time worrying as well. You may not think you're under stress, but all stress sensors are active. Unless you're totally insensitive to your own feelings, as well as others, only option 4 is the correct choice.

Conference Tips

1. Meet co-workers at the first breakfast and review sessions. It's okay to plan different sessions to get the most out of the conference for the company. If you're not a breakfast person, let people know and arrange session reviews at a different time for successive days.

J. FLAGG

2. Arrange dinner times if you don't plan to meet again during the day. You should never leave one person out unless he or she absolutely insists.

3. Social activities vary from conference to conference and should be discussed prior to attending. Don't make people feel like an afterthought on the day of the activity. If you've made personal plans before leaving for the conference, let others know so that they're free to make their own plans.

4. Many conference sessions offer printed notes for a fee. This doesn't mean notes in lieu of attending the session. They are especially helpful in supporting the presentation and for note taking. You'll add value to your attendance by sharing the notes with co-workers when returning to the job.

5. Conference expenses don't need to be on the high side. Most sponsors include breakfast and lunch. Session breaks typically offer a variety of fruits, pastry, juice and coffee. Afternoon sessions

are complete with soft drinks, ice cream, popcorn, and similar snacks. Don't splurge on breakfast and lunch when the conference sponsor is kicking in a good portion of the food expenses. Your company is paying for all those extras in your enrollment fee.

6. The conference typically offers one free day or afternoon. Many of us don't like being pinned down at the hotel, so we rent cars for the week. Later we find that the free day is the only time the car is actually used. Today, many hotels offer car rental services on site, either privately or through a rental dealer. Check with your hotel prior to arriving to inquire about one-day rental alternatives or other transportation made available by the hotel. You'll save money by planning your trip in advance. However, if you're a high control-oriented person, we know you're still going to spend the money to have a car waiting for you all week in the parking lot.

Hotel Tips

We don't mean the section title to be a play on words, but read on to discover what it costs you to check into a hotel. We'll follow through with some helpful travel guidelines as we go along.

You've just left your cab or hotel transport and read all the signs saying, "We accept tips." So you dutifully provide a 20 percent tip on your $25 fare. You're not sure what to give to the driver of a hotel transport because your round-trip ticket cost you a reduced rate or no fee at all, as a service of the hotel. You know the $2.00 you gave is not enough when the driver throws your bag in the gutter. Now a bellman greets you in his neatly pressed uniform and with a smile from ear to ear carries your bags to the check-in counter. After what you just experienced with your transport driver, you slip the bellman $3.00. You just made his day! Well, now you're checked in after sipping complimentary champagne, and don't you feel grand? Now who comes up to grab your bag to take it to your room but a second bellman? You get to your room and discover you only have a few quarters and a $5.00 bill left in small change. While you're contemplating what to give this guy, he starts talking with you while he's turning on the air conditioner. He is quickly filling you in on where the vending machines are and how to use the cooling/heating system, how to call for room service, and telling you what interesting things are going on in the hotel that evening. And, "Oh, don't forget to ask for me if you need anything; my name is Adam," he lets you know. Well, you know you just lost that $5.00 in your pocket.

Helpful Hints

1. Don't be intimidated when giving a tip. A general rule is 15 to 20 percent on priced service. No fee services are at your discretion. You may wish to determine the value of the service and tip equal to any priced fee.

1. After checking in, try to carry your own luggage to the room if you can handle it. This should be considered from a financial, as well as, from a security perspective.

2. If you need assistance to your room, stand in the hall while the bellman carries your bags in. Never enter the room

with him, and never give personal information about yourself. If he invites you in to show you something with the room, let him know you're familiar with whatever it is and stay outside the door. A single dollar per bag is an acceptable tip. Four quarters is still U.S. currency. Don't be intimidated into not using change.

3. Once inside your room, don't open the door to people claiming to be from maintenance or hotel security. Call the front desk and ask for verification that someone has been sent up to check on the room. Ask for a supervisor to accompany the person if you feel at all threatened by the event. Calls to your room indicating that someone is coming up to your room should follow the same procedure. Call the front desk back and verify that they are sending someone and ask for a supervisor to accompany the person.

4. Beware the mini-bar and its convenience. Many hotels have small convenience stores for snacks and beverages. It's only a short trip down the elevator

to save several dollars. You'll notice the small refrigerator in your room provides little space for anything you may bring into the room. Plan accordingly.

5. Many hotels charge a surcharge for telephone usage, even for credit card or 800 number calls. For business travelers this surcharge can quickly lead to large revenues for the hotel and big expenses for your company. Plan your business calls from a public phone where possible.

Traveling with Customers

You're given an opportunity to accompany your customer to further evaluate your product out of state and your sale hangs on your product, as well as on your personal persuasiveness. What do you do?

1. Impress the hell out of them with everything from travel arrangements, presentations, restaurants, hotel selections, and entertainment. Worry about expenses later.

2. Tell your customer where to meet you and when, leaving travel and accommodations up to them, while you make your own travel plans.

3. Meet with your customer before leaving and explain your company policy for customer expenses during travel. Sales-related versus informational trip policy may vary from company to company. Set expectations prior to the trip to avoid misunderstandings.

Depending on the objective of the trip, answer A may be well suited to your business goal. The end result may far exceed any expense incurred as a means of obtaining business. More often than not, answer 3 is the appropriate action. Every company operates within procedural boundaries concerning travel and expenses. It's a good idea to explain to your customer the exact arrangements that you are allowed to handle. Regardless of who is going to pay for actual hotel and air fares, arrangements should be synchronized with the customer in order to provide the attention your customer deserves. Being with them to handle smaller details of ground transportation and various tips along the way can leave a larger impression than meeting your customers at the place of destination.

Customer Travel Tips

1. If your customers have been to the city before, find out if they have hotel or restaurant preferences. Try to fit them into the travel plans.

2. When your customer has no preferences and no avoidance of certain foods, select restaurants of reputation for the area. Your choice can vary from fine dining to casual, especially if the restaurant is unique in some way and popular for that area. For example, if you know a great country restaurant where bells sound when a customer enters wearing a suit and the customer is handed a cowboy hat in exchange for his jacket, your guest is certainly going to remember that night.

3. Never suggest places known for strictly adult entertainment. Read into this what you will. If your customer suggests something more exciting, and it is

against your personal morals, you now have a serious choice to make. Our recommendation is to let your conscience be your guide. If you know in advance that this is the sort of entertainment your client would be looking for, arrange for others to join you that evening who will allow you to leave your client with them after dinner.

4. Plan the itinerary in advance. If your customer is scheduled to meet people at certain times, be sure to have those folks available. Your customer will get very uneasy if he has to wait for people to arrive in the conference room. Even if that person is the president of your company, keeping the customer waiting gives the impression that your time is more valuable than theirs. Not good!

5. Plan the business day without long gaps between activities. If your customer requires private time to check in at work, arrange for that time in the schedule and provide a private area for the customer to work. When the meeting is at a third party location, perhaps at another customer site, serve as the

liaison with your contact there to ensure similar protocol, just as if it were at your own company.

6. When you are the guest of the customer in order to learn more of how their business could benefit from your product or service, accept travel arrangements they may provide on your behalf. But don't expect it, and offer to pick up as many of the expenses as you normally would. Know the company culture, especially in international relationships, to determine proper protocol in accepting customer-purchased flight and accommodations. In some cultures you would insult them by not allowing them to provide for your stay. As a general rule, you should offer to pay your own way unless your customers insist on alternatives.

IT GOES WITH (OUT) SAYING, "WHEN IN ROME, DO AS THE ROMANS DO." We've heard salespeople say that they've switched personalities so many times that they don't know what they're really like anymore. Whether you're in sales or not, people who can adapt to their environment have achieved a great personal asset. Some of us have to work at social flexibility, while the rest of us just seem to have been born with the natural ability to fit any situation. We think the best salespeople, and managers, are those who possess chameleon-like personalities who can act positively in just about any environment and who enjoy conversations with many different personality types. For example: a sales manager was at a dinner gathering with customers and moved to different positions at the table throughout the evening to speak to the various key people. This person truly was a chameleon in disguise. When with the more sober people, he was right on target with facts, business solutions, and sports subjects. The salesperson moved graciously to the other end of the table to sit with another key individual who was obviously feeling the cocktails. The salesperson changed instantly to appear intoxicated as well. He put his arm on the customer's shoulder, began slurring and calling the customer "buddy." The two were instant buddies and were getting deep into a drunken conversation about what was "really" wrong with the company and what was "really" needed to fix the problems. At the end of the conversation, the salesperson went back to the head of the table and delivered a perfectly sober speech on how his company could form the perfect partnership to solve the business problems the customers were experiencing. This salesperson learned the importance of chameleonlike actions to improve his business relationship. Is it deceitful or just good communication skills? You'll have to be the judge of that.

International Travel

As the world moves closer together, learning many cultures, customs, and social etiquette will prove a valuable lesson to the global career-bound workforce. When your business takes you to Rome, Tokyo, or Timbuktu, it's a good idea to brush up on the negotiating power structures and social skills inherent in each culture. Visit your library or local bookstore; there is a wide range of books available for international relations and country related information. Don't make the mistake of relying on your basic skills when leaving the country. What is the right thing to do in your country may be very wrong in another.

Doing as "they" do, whoever "they" are, should go without saying. You'd be surprised at how many business deals have failed due to overconfident reliance on past successes of a superstar in one country being transported to another culture only to discover the same tactics don't work.

Don't go overboard in your preparation by

learning the local language for the country you're visiting. It helps to understand some basic words, but unless you can speak the language fluently, it is recommended not to speak it at all. For one thing you'll embarrass yourself, and worse you may insult the people you are meeting with if you inadvertently use the wrong words. If the folks you're meeting with can't speak your language fluently as well, arrange for an interpreter to accompany both parties. It is only important to know some basic phrases to help you in public situations, such as how to let the taxi driver know where you are staying. At least learn in the local language, "Do you speak English?" If you hear the response: "Qui, or Si, or Ya," then don't forget to start speaking English!

The world is certainly becoming smaller and as cultures collide, all of us need to be more customer conscious. Relying on one set of values and one way of doing things is outdated thinking in a world where multinational corporations are growing faster than an annual crop. To compete in this market, you need to prepare yourself for the journey. The place to begin is within you. If you're headed toward Rome, learn what makes Roman a Roman.

International Travel Tips

1. Always carry your passport with you. When making personal purchases, you qualify for a refund on any country tax you may incur. You will need your passport to obtain the exemption or to obtain the proper paperwork for refunds.

2. Write down where you are staying on a pocket-size card. If you are in a situation in which you need to catch a cab, and there is a language barrier, show the driver the address rather than trying to pronounce it.

3. Many European fares include the gratuity. Read the signs posted in the taxis. When you reach your destination, ask for a receipt. "Do you have a receipt?" is another good phrase to learn in the local language prior to your trip. Tips are appropriate in the 10 to 15 percent range.

4. Within the country, inquire as to the best means for getting around. You'll find that subways can be a positive experience in many European cities.

5. Many restaurants provide menus in the local language and English. If you are traveling alone, it may be a good idea to look at the menu prior to taking your seat. Even if you are presented with the local language menu, you may ask the waiter if they have an English menu available. Very often the waiter/waitress can translate the menu into English for you if it is written in only the local language. When all else fails, remember we do see more and more McDonald's and Burger Kings in many countries.

6. Gratuities in many restaurants are included in the bill. Review your receipt prior to paying. Know the customs of the country you're in. For example, tipping in local pubs is not always acceptable and can be an insult to the establishment.

7. Electrical outlets vary from country to country. Bring as few electrical appliances as possible. Adapters are not always reliable either, so it is a good idea to use hair dryers or irons provided by

the hotels. For extended stays, purchase your appliance once you're in the country. It is much less aggravating!!

8. You wouldn't believe how easy it is to forget your manners when traveling. When approaching a check-in counter at a hotel, you are usually greeted with a warm welcome from the clerk. So often we jump right into the conversation without returning the greeting. Always return a greeting.

9. Currency exchange is available at most airports. Try to judge what you will need ahead of time so you won't be caught short during your trip. Always know what is equivalent to the dollar before entering the country so there won't be any surprises when your cab ride shows up in the hundreds or thousands in the local currency. This will help also in knowing what size tip to provide right away!

Anatomy of a Merger

The years surrounding Millennium 2000 may well go down in history as the era of the corporate merger. Global competition has caused some of the largest mergers in recent history from telecommunication companies, automobile manufacturers, banks, insurance companies, to countless other industries. Everyone recognizes the importance of the merger for the betterment of the company and the strategic value in remaining competitive. But what is it doing to the workforce, and how does it affect you, the worker?

It starts with management presentations at corporate meetings on the state of the current situation for the company. Explanations are provided of what it will take to remain competitive. First, you may see the curtailing of certain expenditures, office closures, and a hiring freeze. You wonder how this can happen in a growing economy, when you have more work to do than before, and electronic processes replace manual procedures on an ever-increasing basis.

In your heart you know you need more skilled workers and not just the giving of more work to those around you. Then something begins to happen. The rumor mill.

The rumors begin like a perfect ring, there is no beginning and no end, and they just go round and round. People begin asking questions like, "Have you heard anything about a merger?" Then statements are heard, such as, "Have you heard that the CEOs from this company and that one have been meeting on a regular basis." Then you might learn that there was a secret meeting of the board of directors at an undisclosed location, but you know it was in Chicago. Finally, the CEO calls a meeting to dispel any rumor of a merger. Now, you really know something is going on! After this meeting, start buying stock, something is going to happen.

Finally, an announcement is made in the form of a letter delivered to every employee's workstation. You learn that for many years it has been recognized that to stay globally competitive the company must strategically align resources with one or more companies. You are assured in the memo that it will make for a stronger company and one offering more jobs and more opportunities for all employees. Of course, there will be some redundancy in positions, but those will be evaluated carefully and consultants will be utilized to ensure fairness and perhaps some equality between the merged companies. In other words, don't worry, be happy!

All productivity for the day just went out the window. People are huddled in groups of two or more discussing the memo, interjecting their own spin on how the company will change, who wins and who loses, and already worrying about what this means to them. Every emotion, every possibility, every negative outcome is experienced in this first half day of the announcement. It doesn't matter how great things will turn out for the company when it might mean that some persons can no longer support themselves or their families. Fear starts from the beginning and stays with you until you know for sure how this merger will impact you personally. This is reality.

The company recognizes the personal aspect of mergers on their employees, so they go out and hire the best consultants, they provide merger-related material to give to their employees, and they hold several meetings to try to put minds at ease. The truth is that these activities only add fuel to an already blazing fire of worry. Today's workforce is an educated body of people who believe that these tactics are only propaganda and they realize that no matter what training they are provided with on mergers, only one thing matters. How will this affect me?

The problem with mergers is that they take months or years to fully complete. The legal procedures must be satisfied before announcements can be made concerning the new management team. Once the management team is announced, only then can the rest of the organization be developed. This is the time when all hell breaks loose and you see true human nature at work. If you thought office politics were bad before an announced merger, they are worse afterwards. All the characteristics of the Caesars, weasels, wannabes, defenders, and gladiators come right out and stare you in the face. The new factions are those now from the merged company. You are introduced to people from the other companies slowly and their personality traits are not readily visible to you on first introductions. These new players appear as people you can really like and would like to work with in the future. The truth is you can't assess how you will work with them until a closer working relationship develops.

You will also witness friends turning against each other and the true colors of those only interested in themselves brilliantly shine forth. The saddest part in all of this is that it begins at the top and rolls downhill. Positions are selected for the senior management jobs first, so all the worst of the powerplays are witnessed by staff members first hand. The culture for the new company begins to evolve with each new selection. When you witness who the people are who are getting appointments, the shifting of sides begins at the lower levels. The winners and losers start to shape the new organization and the culture. The staff has just witnessed the ugliest battle away from any known war. Now it is their turn to worry as interviews begin at their level. Because the merger will take some time to complete, they will be secure for a year or two, but redundant positions will eventually be eliminated.

The side effect of a merger on lower positions is the weeding out of those who are considered poor performers, assumed troublemakers, people management just doesn't like, and those who are just considered odd. For during a merger, a company can come up with just about any excuse to eliminate jobs legally if they do it right. Unfortunately, very qualified personnel are also let go because of political favors, for example, a manager appointed in the merger is protecting an associate from his/her previous organization and displaces the counterpart from the oppositely merged company regardless of qualifications.

There is no easy recommendation to survive through a merger since each company and culture drives the motivation aspects differently. The wise thing is to be yourself and continue to do the work you were hired to do for the company. If there is witch hunting and weeding out going on, that is out of your control, stay out of the rumor mill and the groups congregating that are drawing their own conclusions. There are people out there ready to pass along information that they hear in these groups and you don't want to be caught in the crossfire.

One thing is certain. During the interviewing process, you may be asked to provide an assessment of your manager, other managers, and your co-workers. Be diplomatic here and don't speak negatively about anyone unless there is true cause to do so. Those interviewing are looking for any stake to place in the ground to come up with underlying reasons to remove someone. Remember that what you say about others may be the very thing that they are saying about you. You must let your conscience be your guide in all you say and do.

When the decisions are finally made and staff is in place, the environment will be different and not always for the best. If you were selected to remain, you're going to be comparing the new organization to the old and you will need to reassess how you fit into this new company. Old questions about staying or leaving will again be on the forefront of your mind. Read this book again and see how it fits in to your new environment.

If you were one of those out-placed, you will feel the anger and rage that is associated with suddenly being out of work. Let it happen. Losing a job is a mournful experience. Soon you will begin to count your blessings. Look at the situation for what it was, understand where you were in the company, how you really fit into the situation, and ask yourself if you were really happy there. Chances are you weren't. If you are not sure, take out a piece of paper and on one side list all the things you liked about the job or company, and on the other side list those things you didn't like. Be sure you include your emotional feelings as well as the material aspects of working for the pre-merged and merged company.

Losing a job is listed as one of the highest causes of stress, right up there with losing a loved one and having financial problems. If losing your job is making coping difficult, seek out professional help from the medical and legal fields. A doctor will help you work through the emotional stress and offer assistance in helping you cope with the turmoil in your life. A lawyer can be consulted if you believe there was unjust cause for your termination. Even if there is no legal recourse, a lawyer can be useful to help you understand what avenues to take going forward. You may also require legal assistance for unemployment claims in some circumstances. For example, a company may ask you to stay on until a merger is completed, but the circumstances place you in a difficult situation, making it unbearable to stay on for any amount of time. There is legal recourse for situations and it will be worth your time to investigate them before doing anything rash.

One thing you may learn is that it is not worth your health to stay in a position that makes you feel oppressed, harassed, or threatened. A company cannot take away your self-respect if you don't let them.

There is a saying that there are only two things certain in life: death and taxes. Some people believed that there was a third, the company they worked for since it brought them through retirement and pension plans. There are few companies today that can offer that security. What you are left with has to be faith in yourself to provide for your own future security. Although a job does not define who you really are, it is a major part of your existence and working through change is a difficult time for any person. You may find that the decision process alone is the worst stress you'll experience. Once you make the decision to change, you may find the road to recovery is a new job or a new career. Good luck.

Parting Thoughts

Today is no different from the past in that it is always changing. The world could be a pleasant place to live in, if only people learn to get along with each other. For no matter how bright the business prospect is in a growing global economy, we still see wars, famine, and prejudice within our countries. The imbalance in human living conditions is still far too extreme for hopes of a utopian society. But for those of you fortunate enough to be participating in a progressive business industry, you have a great opportunity to make a difference in your corner of the world.

How you choose to participate is a personal decision. It isn't about winning or losing, or playing the game versus sitting on the bench, it's about living and enjoying life in an atmosphere of cooperation, shared experiences, seeking goals that bring you closer to meeting your personal requirements. For in the end, all we can look back on is how we feel about ourselves and the way we managed our own lives. To get along in this life, we are all prisoners of work. Our economy thrives on supply and demand and the money that is derived from the exchange between households and business. Since it is our own household and our personal well-being and growth of wealth that is at the heart of our economy, we need to work. We need to work well with each other and for each other and feel good about what we're doing.

Sorry is the person who in the end can only say, "I should have . . ., I could have . . ., if only I'd . . ., if they hadn't . . . I'd have. . . ." Life tests and demands many things from us, but the true test may be in how we deal with others as we seek to find our place in the world.

Don't just seize the todays; seize the tomorrows by shaping the environment in which you plan to work and play throughout your life. We are all connected as humans, as persons wanting to live better, as explorers through time in our own space and in our home, this place we call The World.

J. FLAGG

J. FLAGG

Note from the Author

Thank you for purchasing and reading *P.O.W.: Prisoners of Work*. You are invited to submit comments or original stories about your own work experience to support the topics introduced within this work guide.

Information received will be considered for inclusion into a second edition. You may write to the author at *GIROUARD@visto.com*.

All correspondence must include your full name and address in the body of the text. If your material is selected for print, you will be sent a release form prior to publishing.